W9-BQU-602

ANCIENT ROME

Virginia Loh-Hagan

45TH PARALLEL PRESS

Published in the United States of America by Cherry Lake Publishing Group
Ann Arbor, Michigan
www.cherrylakepublishing.com
Reading Adviser: Marla Conn, MS, Ed., Literacy specialist, Read-Ability, Inc.

Book Designer: Melinda Millward

Photo Credits: © Serhii Bobyk/Shutterstock.com, cover, 1; © Masterlevsha/Shutterstock.com, 4; © Album / Alamy Stock Photo, 6; © emperorcosar/Shutterstock.com, 8; © Fotokvadrat/Shutterstock.com, back cover, 10; © duncan1890/istockphoto.com, 12, 20; © vukkostic Adobe Stock, 14; © rudall30/Shutterstock.com, 16; © bauhaus1000/istockphoto.com, 18; © García Juan/Dreamstime.com, 22; © wjarek/Shutterstock.com, 24; © Chronicle / Alamy Stock Photo , 27; © ZU_09/istockphoto.com, 28

Graphic Element Credits: © Milos Djapovic/Shutterstock.com, back cover, front cover; © cajoer/Shutterstock.com, back cover, front cover, multiple interior pages; © GUSAK OLENA/Shutterstock.com, back cover, multiple interior pages; © Miloje/Shutterstock.com, front cover; © Rtstudio/Shutterstock.com, multiple interior pages; © Konstantin Nikiteev/Dreamstime.com, 29

Library of Congress Cataloging-in-Publication Data

Names: Loh-Hagan, Virginia, author.
Title: Ancient Rome / by Virginia Loh-Hagan.
Description: Ann Arbor, Michigan : Cherry Lake Publishing, [2021] | Series: Surviving history | Includes bibliographical references and index.
Identifiers: LCCN 2020003279 (print) | LCCN 2020003280 (ebook) | ISBN 9781534169081 (hardcover) | ISBN 9781534170766 (paperback) | ISBN 9781534172609 (pdf) | ISBN 9781534174443 (ebook)
Subjects: LCSH: Rome—Civilization—Juvenile literature. | Rome—History—Juvenile literature.
Classification: LCC DG77 .L65 2021 (print) | LCC DG77 (ebook) | DDC 937—dc23
LC record available at https://lccn.loc.gov/2020003279
LC ebook record available at https://lccn.loc.gov/2020003280

Printed in the United States of America
Corporate Graphics

TABLE OF CONTENTS

INTRODUCTION

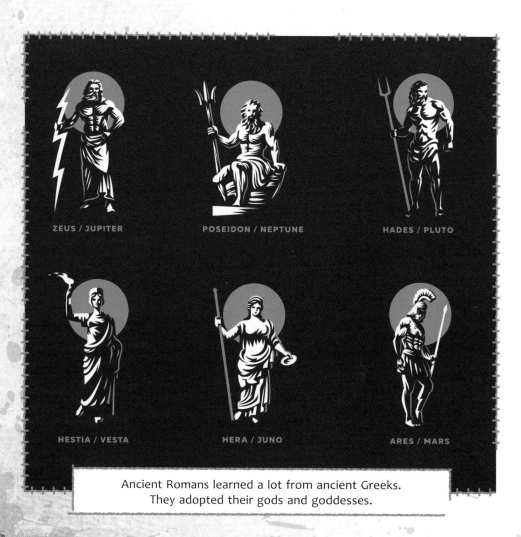

ZEUS / JUPITER

POSEIDON / NEPTUNE

HADES / PLUTO

HESTIA / VESTA

HERA / JUNO

ARES / MARS

Ancient Romans learned a lot from ancient Greeks.
They adopted their gods and goddesses.

A group of villages developed along Italy's Tiber River. Around 750 BCE, the villages joined together. They formed a city called Rome.

At first, kings ruled **ancient** Rome. Ancient means from a time long ago. Then, Rome became a **republic**. A republic is a type of government. People elect other people to represent them. Ancient Romans formed a **senate**. A senate is a group of elected officials. This group made decisions for ancient Rome.

Most senators were **patricians**. Patricians were people from noble classes. **Plebeians** were working-class people. They could vote. But they couldn't be city leaders. Then, in 287 BCE, plebeians got the same rights as patricians. In general, the rich lived better than the poor.

Barbarian tribes invaded ancient Rome.

The ancient Roman republic and army grew. Rome conquered new lands. With power came problems. Ancient Romans became greedy. They relied on **slaves**. Slaves are people who are forced to work without pay.

Julius Caesar was a Roman general. He took over power. In 31 BCE, ancient Rome became an **empire**. Empires are several countries ruled by one leader. Caesar's adopted son, Augustus, became the first Roman emperor. Augustus brought peace to Rome. Ancient Romans did great things. They grew trade. They built roads. They built great buildings. They wrote great literature. They improved law. They improved politics. They improved the military.

However, there were more wars. There was more greed. Christianity spread. The Roman Empire fell.

FIGHT OR NO FIGHT?

The Colosseum is a famous arena. It's in Rome. On its opening day, over 9,000 animals were killed.

Gladiators were trained fighters. They fought against other gladiators. They fought against wild animals. They fought in **arenas**. Arenas are areas for public events. Gladiators fought to entertain people. They fought to the death. These fights were called games or bloodsports. This took place for 1,000 years.

Ancient Roman nobles used gladiator fights to gain the love of the people. They promoted themselves. Gladiators made a lot of money for trainers and owners.

Most gladiators were slaves. They fought to make money for their masters. Some fought to buy their freedom. Some gladiators were prisoners of war. Some were **criminals**. Criminals are people who break laws.

QUESTION 1

Which type of gladiator would you have been?

A You fought on **chariots**. Chariots were wheeled carts pulled by animals. You had a driver. You used weapons while in the chariot.

B You fought in pairs. You had a fighting partner. You defended each other. You attacked as a team.

C You fought alone. You were matched with a fighter of your size. But you had to fight by yourself.

There were gladiator schools. Gladiators learned to fight. They were taught to hurt, not kill.

SURVIVAL TOOLS

Gladiators fought with a gladius sword. This sword was made from iron. It had two sharp edges. This was for cutting and chopping. The sword also narrowed down to a point. This was good for stabbing and thrusting. The handle had a solid grip. It had ridges for fingers. This gave gladiators good balance to slash with great force. A rudis was a wooden gladius sword. Gladiators practiced fighting with a rudis. They used a rudis to protect themselves. They wanted to avoid serious injuries. They also used a rudis to protect their gladius swords. They didn't want to damage their swords. A rudis was given to winners of a battle. It was also given to retired gladiators. These gladiators survived the battles. They earned their freedom.

WAR OR PEACE?

Ancient Romans were always ready for war. They had a centralized command. They had supplies.

Ancient Romans fought many wars. They fought for power. They fought to expand their empire. They fought to protect their lands. Ancient Roman soldiers were known for their skills. They were well-trained. They were feared.

Ancient Rome's armed forces were made up of **legions**. Legions are military groups. Legions cost a lot of money. But they brought riches to the city. They brought lands. They brought treasures. They also brought slaves.

Marcus Aurelius was a Roman emperor. He commanded many wars. He fought for control over lands in the East. He fought against Persians. He also fought against Germans. Germans attacked Rome.

Soldiers got rewards. But disloyal soldiers were punished. Some were clubbed to death. Some were sold into slavery.

QUESTION 2

Which Roman legion would you have joined?

A The **equites**. Equites are soldiers who fight on horses. This was the most well-respected group. Rich young men became equites. They bought their own weapons and horses.

B The **infantry**. Infantry are foot soldiers. They're the main soldiers. They bought their own weapons. The newest soldiers fought at the front. The more skilled soldiers were the second line. **Veterans** were the third line. Veterans are experienced soldiers.

C The **velites**. Velites were light infantry. They were poor. They couldn't afford to buy all their gear. They mainly fought with darts and short swords.

Ancient Roman soldiers swore loyalty to the leader. Only men ages 18 to 60 served as soldiers.

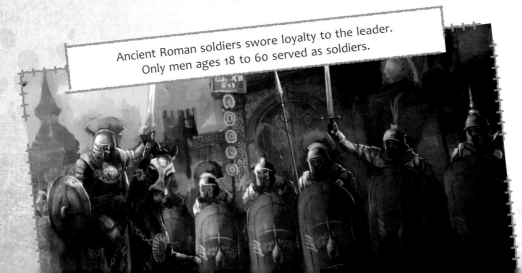

SURVIVAL BY THE NUMBERS

- Ancient Romans hosted chariot races. These races could be dangerous. Gaius Appuleius Diocles was a chariot racer. He won 1,462 of the 4,257 races. He raced for 24 years. He earned about 35,863,120 sesterces. The sesterce was an ancient Roman coin. This equals $15 billion in today's money. Diocles is thought to be the highest-paid athlete of all time.
- About 28 percent of ancient Roman babies died within the first year of life.
- About 50 percent of ancient Romans died by age 5. Of those still alive at age 10, about 50 percent would die by the age of 50.
- About 400,000 people and over 1 million animals died in the Colosseum.
- The Battle of Cannae happened in 216 BCE. Hannibal invaded Rome. Rome lost. About 50,000 to 70,000 Roman soldiers were killed. This battle is used as an example of the perfect defeat of an enemy army.

TO KILL OR NOT TO KILL?

"Beware the Ides of March" is a famous saying.

Assassination is the killing of someone for political reasons. Some of the most famous assassinations took place in ancient Rome.

Julius Caesar was assassinated. Senators thought he was becoming too powerful. They stabbed him 23 times. They killed him on March 15. This date was called "the Ides of March." His death meant the end of the Roman republic.

Ancient Rome was a dangerous place to be an emperor. About 20 percent of ancient Rome's emperors were assassinated while in power. Some experts blamed the rain. Without rain, there were no crops or food. People starved. They were mad at their leaders.

QUESTION 3

What role would you have played in ancient Roman society?

A You were an ancient Roman citizen. This class included noble people. It included rich landowners. Citizens could vote. They could own property. They could run for public office.

B You were an ancient Roman senator. Senators had a lot of power. They made the laws. But they had to follow rules. They needed permission to leave Italy. They couldn't own ships.

C You were an ancient Roman emperor. Emperors controlled the legions. They needed senate support to rule. They fought hard to keep their power.

Children took the status of their parents.

SURVIVOR BIOGRAPHY

Julia Agrippina is also known as Agrippina the Younger. She was an ancient Roman noble. She lived from 15 to 59 CE. She was the great-granddaughter of Emperor Augustus. She was accused of trying to kill her brother, who was Emperor Caligula. She was banned from Rome. She returned to Rome when Caligula died. She married Gnaeus Domitius Ahenobarbus. She had her son, Nero, with him. After her husband died, she married Emperor Claudius, who was her uncle. She had him adopt Nero as his heir. She became the first empress of Rome. She was very powerful. Some experts say she poisoned Claudius. She did this to make her son, Nero, an emperor. She ruled Rome through Nero. Nero grew more powerful. He took away Agrippina's powers. He tried to kill her. He put her in a boat designed to sink. Agrippina survived. She swam ashore. Nero tried again. He had a soldier stab her to death.

SICK OR HEALTHY?

The Antonine and Cyprian plagues may have been similar to smallpox and measles.

Soldiers fought wars in foreign places. They came back. They brought sicknesses with them. The Antonine **plague** lasted from 165 to 180 CE. Plagues are sicknesses that spread quickly. The Cyprian plague lasted from 250 to 270 CE. The plagues killed about 2,000 people a day. They killed one-third of ancient Romans.

Many people lived in Rome. They were crammed into small spaces. They didn't have clean water. Their human waste was in the street. This meant sicknesses spread. Many ancient Romans got **cholera**. Cholera is a sickness that makes people throw up and poop a lot.

QUESTION 4

What would have been your risk of getting sick?

A You were part of the ruling class. You were born into this class. You lived in a big house. You had access to doctors.

B You had a job. But you weren't rich. You might have been in contact with sick people.

C You were an ancient Roman soldier. You might have gotten sick while fighting. You got the sickness directly. You spread it to others. Plagues killed many soldiers. This decreased the power of the military.

The Antonine plague was also called the plague of Galen. Galen was the doctor who discovered it.

SURVIVAL TIPS

Follow these tips to survive a cholera outbreak.

- Drink safe water. Use water that has been boiled. Use bottled water.
- Avoid ice that wasn't made with safe water.
- Wash your hands often. Wash with soap and safe water.
- Brush your teeth with safe water.
- Wash anything you use for cooking and eating with safe water.
- Cook food well. Don't eat raw seafood. Keep food covered. Eat food hot.
- Peel fruits and vegetables. Cook vegetables.
- Keep areas clean. Clean the kitchen. Clean the bathroom. Clean the laundry room.
- Get information from the Centers for Disease Control and Prevention. Don't travel to places with cholera outbreaks.
- Repair wells. Improve the supply of clean water.

BREAD OR MEAT?

For meat, ancient Romans ate eggs, hare, snails, small birds, boar, and seafood.

Many ancient Romans may have died from **malnutrition**. Malnutrition is a lack of food. Ancient Roman diets weren't balanced.

Ancient Romans ate a lot of grains. Poor people were given monthly supplies of grain. They ate dried peas. They ate grains in **porridges**. Porridges are boiled cereal. Not many ancient Romans had ovens. This meant only rich people ate bread. They bought bread from bakers.

Ancient Romans ate little meat. Meat was usually boiled. Or it was fried. As the empire grew, ancient Romans ate more fruits and vegetables.

Ancient Romans didn't check their foods. So, many foods may have been **contaminated**. Contaminated means it could make them sick.

QUESTION 5

How would you have eaten?

A You were working class. You grew your own food. You didn't eat too much. You ate what you needed.

B You were rich. You bought meat. You bought sweets. You bought milk. Rich Romans were known for hosting feasts. They ate a lot. Then, they threw up. They did this to make room to eat more.

C You were poor. You ate a lot of **millet**. Millet is a cereal. It's used for animal food. You drank from the Tiber River. The river water may have been contaminated.

Ancient Romans mainly ate foods from their local areas.

SURVIVAL RESULTS

The fall of Rome started the Dark Ages in Europe.

Would you have survived?

Find out! Add up your answers to the chapter questions. Did you have more **A**s, **B**s, or **C**s?

- If you had more **A**s, then you're a survivor! Congrats!

- If you had more **B**s, then you're on the edge. With some luck, you might have just made it.

- If you had more **C**s, then you wouldn't have survived.

Are you happy with your results? Did you have a tie? Sometimes fate is already decided for us. Follow the link below to our webpage. Scroll until you find the series name *Surviving History*. Click download. Print out the template. Follow the directions to create your own paper die. Read the book again. Roll the die to find your new answers. Did your fate change?

https://cherrylakepublishing.com/teaching_guides

DIGGING DEEPER: DID YOU KNOW...?

Ancient Rome was exciting. People achieved great things. But many lives were lost as well. Surviving history involves many different factors. Dig deeper. Consider some of the facts below.

QUESTION 1:

Which type of gladiator would you have been?

- Some gladiators fought on horses. They could move faster.
- Gladiators were skilled in different types of weapons.
- Mostly men were gladiators. There were a few women gladiators. They were called gladiatrix.

QUESTION 2:

Which Roman legion would you have joined?

- Equites charged through enemy lines. Some would get off their horses. They'd fight on the ground.
- Infantry had helmets, shields, armor, and long swords.
- Velites didn't wear armor. They served as scouts.

QUESTION 3:

What role would you have played in ancient Roman society?

- Non-citizens were slaves. They had no rights.
- Senators wore special robes. They wore a special ring. They wore special shoes.
- Emperors didn't see themselves as kings.

QUESTION 4:

What would have been your risk of getting sick?

- Ancient Roman doctors learned from the ancient Greeks.
- Ancient Romans didn't have toilet paper. They used a stick with a sponge. They shared this.
- Soldiers spent a lot of time with other soldiers. This spread germs.

QUESTION 5:

How would you have eaten?

- Many ancient Romans ate cheese, especially the poor and soldiers.
- Rich Romans could add flavors to their breads.
- Ancient Romans used fish sauces. This helped season their food.

GLOSSARY

ancient (AYN-shuhnt) from a time long ago

arenas (uh-REE-nuhz) areas used for public events

assassination (uh-sas-uh-NAY-shuhn) killing of someone for political reasons

chariots (CHAR-ee-uhts) wheeled carts pulled by large animals

cholera (KAH-lur-uh) sickness of the small intestine that causes vomiting and diarrhea

contaminated (kuhn-TAM-uh-nay-tid) poisoned or polluted

criminals (KRIM-uh-nuhlz) people who break laws

empire (EM-pire) a group of nations ruled by one leader

equites (EK-wih-tays) soldiers who fight on horses

gladiators (GLAD-ee-ay-turz) trained ancient Roman fighters

infantry (IN-fuhn-tree) foot soldiers

legions (LEE-juhnz) ancient Rome's armed forces

malnutrition (mal-noo-TRISH-uhn) extreme lack of food

millet (MIL-it) fast-growing cereal plant that is grown in warm countries and in areas with poor soil

patricians (puh-TRISH-uhnz) people from noble classes

plague (PLAYG) a sickness that could spread quickly

plebeians (PLEE-bee-uhnz) working-class people

porridges (POR-ij-iz) boiled cereals like oatmeal

republic (rih-PUHB-lik) a type of government where elected representatives hold the power

senate (SEN-it) a group of elected officials that makes laws

slaves (SLAYVZ) people who are forced to work for free

velites (VIH-lites) light infantry who mainly served as scouts

veterans (VET-ur-uhnz) experienced soldiers

LEARN MORE!

- Klar, Jeremy. *The Totally Gross History of Ancient Rome.* New York, NY: Rosen Central, 2016.
- O'Connor, Jim, and John O'Brien (illust.). *Where Is the Colosseum?* New York, NY: Grosset and Dunlap, 2017.
- Shoulders, Debbie, Michael Shoulders, and Victor Juhasz (illust.). *G Is for Gladiator: An Ancient Rome Alphabet.* Ann Arbor, MI: Sleeping Bear Press, 2010.

INDEX

ABOUT THE AUTHOR

Dr. Virginia Loh-Hagan is an author, university professor, and former classroom teacher. She traveled to Rome. She loved it! She lives in San Diego with her very tall husband and very naughty dogs. To learn more about her, visit www.virginialoh.com.